The Ketch *Ceres*
1811-1936

Charmian Astbury

Published by:
Sappho Publications
43 North Street, Northam, Bideford
North Devon, EX39 1DH

British Library Cataloguing-in-Publication Data.
A catalogue record for this book is available
from the British Library.

Arthur H. Stockwell Ltd., bear no responsibility
for the accuracy of events recorded in this book.

ISBN 0 9539640 2 7
Printed in Great Britain by
Arthur H. Stockwell Ltd.
Torrs Park   Ilfracombe
Devon

Contents and Illustrations   Page No

Foreword

An introduction

Tuesday, 24th November 1936

The *Ceres*:

i) Recollections and records

ii) Episodes and experiences

iii) Trade and the times

iv) Her ballad, legends and legacies

The *Ceres*:

i) Her obituaries

ii) Afterwards

Sources: books, documents and unpublished work   68

Acknowledgments   70

1.The *Ceres* entering Bude in the surf, c.1900

Foreword

Built in order to be able to run onto the shores and beaches of the Westcountry, and elsewhere, the small wooden sailing vessels, the ketches, were a vital part of the nineteenth century economy. The ketch *Ceres*, Official Number 15560, was one such. She survived one hundred and twenty-five years, from 1811 when she was built, until 1936, when she foundered. Her first hundred years were worked under sail alone.

Many ketches kept going for eighty or a hundred years and more. There were a number of key elements to both the ketch economy and their longevity. These elements were family ownership, with family members sailing each vessel, the share system of purchase and the mutual insurance associations, which were local co-operative bodies having little or no overheads. Each individual ketch history provides a small and very real look at the life and times through which each vessel passed.

The existing maritime documents record almost as much of this social history as the actual information set down about each vessel. Such documents are a source of delight to the reader, but one has to be aware that the information so recorded does vary, for all sorts of reasons. A case in point is the recorded figure for the net registered tons of the *Ceres*. She was enlarged once, so one would expect her weight to increase once. However, her weight, or net registered tons, has been recorded as 32, 34, 44, 54, 57 and 58 tons. Generally speaking, should there be two strong sources noting the same figure, then that figure is probably accurate. On this basis, in this book, the *Ceres* weighed 32 tons when built and 44 tons following her enlargement. Similar judgements have had to be made about dates, names, categories and so forth.

This small book is by no means a definitive history of either the ketches as a whole or the *Ceres* herself. The records are the records: any error in the interpretation of those records is the author's own.

Charmian Astbury, March 2004

2. The ketch *Ceres* in the River Torridge, as seen from Appledore
Quay, about 1930

An Introduction

How does a story start? Where does a history begin and end? What is it that happens to make sure that little bits and pieces of information about events, about objects and individuals are saved? Why are such items tucked away with great care and then forgotten until recalled when looking out old photographs? Whatever it is that prompts a person to keep something, more often than not a something destined to lie unremarked throughout several lifetimes, thankfully will always happen. Such small items, most relevant to their own time, can and do start a story, begin or end a history.

By the time the ketch *Ceres* came to the end of her one hundred and twenty-five years in 1936 she was a very well-known vessel indeed. Once it had become apparent that she was outlasting her contemporaries the *Ceres* became something of a legend, something of a celebrity. Her comings and goings were noted with both interest and affection. She featured in newspaper articles and reports. A considerable number of photographs were taken of her. A postcard of her at Bude was produced which also carried a brief history of her life and times. And at her passing not only was a commemorative ballad for her published, but her loss was reported widely in the newspapers of the day.

The ketch *Ceres* was known to me because Walter, father of my old friend Ann, used to talk to me about her. Walter had been on board the *Ceres* the night that she foundered off Baggy Point in North Devon, with eighty tons of slag in her hold. He told me about her age, her work during the Napoleonic Wars of the early nineteenth century, her trade and more, as he sat opposite me at the large table with the glow and warmth of the old Appledore kitchen range behind him. While talking he would be working away on the circular rope mat that he eventually gave me. I recall asking him if a ketch was anything like a fishing boat, a trawler. No, no, it was a sailing vessel with an auxiliary engine. He stowed away his mat-making tools in the table drawer. How could a wooden sailing vessel have survived all that time at sea, working through years of war and years of trade? And why had she been carrying slag? What

9

purpose could those huge quantities of slag have had in this remote area? Well, forty years on from those speculations of mine about her and her role, and nearly two hundred since the *Ceres* herself was first launched, this small book sets out to consider such things and to explore a little more of her life and times.

By the time the twentieth century was well underway the old wooden trading vessels, the ketches, had more or less run their course. During the nineteenth century, a century in which the ketch had contributed significantly to the economy of the South West, large numbers of these small wooden vessels, mostly well under one hundred tons unladen, would be out and about at any one time at sea. They transported anything and everything.

The ketches were designed and built, in the main, on the shores and estuaries of the Westcountry by those who would sail them, to carry goods to those same Westcountry shores and estuaries. They traded between the coastal communities of Cornwall and Devon, of Somerset and South Wales, and those of the coasts of Scotland and Ireland. They reached the east coast ports of Britain and crossed the North Sea to Scandinavia. The ketches could and did trade across the Atlantic to America as well as to the ports of Spain and the Mediterranean.

At the peak of these trading years there would have been at least ten or twelve ketches a year being built, each taking up to two years to build and sometimes longer. Some of these small vessels would turn out to be surprisingly long-lived. Most of the ketches were built during the nineteenth century, though they had first started to evolve during the eighteenth. And there were at least twenty ketches that were built to work in the Westcountry between the years 1900 and 1921. The *Bessie Ellen* was one such, built 1911 and now lovingly restored and today sailing out of Plymouth. Another was the *Dido C*, built in 1921. The *Dido C* would turn out to be the last of the working Westcountry ketches to be built, ending her days at a mere forty-three years of age. A fair number of the ketches reached one hundred years of age. The *Ceres* has, even today, outlived them all.

Tuesday 24ᵗʰ November 1936

It was on the evening of Tuesday 24ᵗʰ November 1936 that the ketch *Ceres* left Swansea in South Wales bound for Bude in North Cornwall with eighty tons of slag in her hold. She had her skipper and her mate aboard. It was to be her final voyage. After one hundred and twenty-five years at sea, with an estimated quarter of a million tons of cargo transported safely over the years to her credit and a superb reputation that would ensure that her passing would be reported worldwide, she foundered off Baggy Point and came to the end of her days. Oswald Jeffery was her skipper that night and Walter Ford, Ann's father, her mate.

The *Ceres* carried six rockets, the matches with which to ignite them and a number of flares. At home in Appledore, Ann's mother heard, at something before ten o'clock, one of the rockets fired that Tuesday night. She always said in later years that she knew beyond any doubt that it was Walter out there. It was late November and had been dark for some hours. The fog was coming down, there was a light breeze blowing and a moderate sea running.

The first rocket had been fired when the deck of the *Ceres* was awash and she was lurching badly as more and more bags of slag became saturated with sea water. The pumps were unable to compete with the inevitability of her sinking. The rowing boat was launched and the two crew abandoned ship. The *Ceres* was off Baggy Point with still some three miles to go to reach the port of Appledore, for which she had been heading anyway because of the worsening weather. Her skipper and her mate kept the rowing boat as near to the *Ceres* as possible. Though sinking steadily the *Ceres* was a far larger object than the

11

rowing boat and was their only real hope of being found at all that night.

How could Ann's mother, Beena, possibly have known that it was Walter out there? There were no radios, no telephones, it was dark, it was foggy, and the two men had had to abandon ship several miles away from a safe haven on a very unforgiving coast. Well, she did know. In fact, she was so certain that it was Walter needing help out there that she went down to her in-laws and told Walter's father that the rocket she had heard was Walter calling. Her father-in-law was astounded. Ann's mother insisted that he go down to the quay for it was Walter calling and he, Walter's father, must be there at the quayside when the lifeboat returned. Her father-in-law looked at her. He was a man with centuries of seafaring in his ancestry. He went down to the quayside and waited for the lifeboat to return. Ann's mother had been right. Walter was on the lifeboat, with his skipper, both soaking wet but otherwise unharmed.

When the returning Appledore lifeboat, the *V.C.S.* with her crew and the two survivors, came alongside the quay around midnight they were welcomed by a crowd of well wishers in spite of the lateness of the hour. Among the crowd on the quay were the vicar of Appledore, who there and then offered prayers for the safe deliverance of the two-man crew, the doctor, whose services thankfully had not been required and Walter's father.

As far as any of the coastal communities were, and still are, concerned, the saving of lives from shipwreck has always been a matter for thanksgiving, both the for endeavour rewarded and for the lives saved, whatever the many stories to the contrary might suggest. Both seamen and volunteers, locals and visitors, would have manned any lifeboat needed. As long as there was one person capable of handling a boat, there would always be willing hands to get the lifeboat launched and to

12

help with any rowing. Such assistance was put on a more regular footing at the beginning of the nineteenth century when the first Appledore Lifeboat was built, financed by the National Shipwreck Local Committee, at a cost of £90. The seventh of the Appledore lifeboats to serve was the *V.C.S.* She would serve for the sixteen years from 1922 to 1938. The *V.C.S.*, the lifeboat which went to the rescue of the *Ceres,* was the first motor lifeboat to serve the Bristol Channel. She had been built by J S White & Co. of Cowes at a cost of £8,162.

The financing of the building of lifeboats has always been by public subscription of one sort or another. The *V.C.S* was financed from three legacies, namely, those of Ellen and James Vagg, Cecilia Marshall and Sarah Sleemin, hence the three initials of her name. The number of rescues achieved in her sixteen years of service was forty and the number of lives saved was forty-one. There were two rescues during November 1936; that of the motor trawler *Clarissa* on 19th, with three lives saved, and that of the *Ceres* on 24th, with two lives saved.

3. The *V.C.S.* and her crew, Appledore, probably 1922

13

The story of that night, as told by Oswald Jeffery in his own words, was published on 26th November 1936 in the *Western Morning News and Daily Gazette*:

'We left Swansea on Tuesday night bound for Bude with a cargo of slag. There was a certain amount of fog, but we were successful in making Bull Lighthouse, and came passed Morte Point into Morte Bay, intending to go in over the Bar for the night as it was too rough to venture on to Bude and a sea was beginning to run with a certain amount of fog added to the story.

'At 8 o'clock I went below to rest for an hour, leaving the mate in charge. An hour later he came below to tell me there was water in the engine room. I rushed to the engine room and found water being splashed about by the couplings of the engine. I was completely soaked, and as I entered the room I found the water almost up to my waist, I went on deck and immediately manned the pumps until I was overtaken by exhaustion.

'Then the mate took over while I went back to the engine room and found that the water, instead of decreasing, was higher than before. We tried to get the ship in over the Bar, but the volume of water made her roll badly, and I gave orders for the ship's rowing boat to be launched.

'I then got the six rockets in the ship and started firing them in the hope of attracting the coastguards at Down End. I succeeded in firing two rockets, but then the ship began to lurch so badly that I found it impossible to light any more rockets with matches. I then had to use flares, a rather risky business as the rockets were likely to explode at once. One exploded a few yards up in the air. I kept one rocket for the ship's boat, and when the water was washing the decks we abandoned the vessel, taking with us the ship's, and other, important papers, but none of our clothes as it was dangerous to go below.

'When in the ship's boat I fixed one rocket between the ribs of the boat and fired. This was evidently seen from Appledore, and we lay in the shelter of the *Ceres* which was fast sinking to await the arrival of the lifeboat. We were taken aboard the lifeboat, which rounded the *Ceres* to see whether she could be towed ashore, but she was too far submerged and we proceeded to Appledore.'

Their distress signal was first seen by the wife of the lifeboat signalman of West Appledore, when she noticed a rocket go up in the direction of Croyde. She at once notified the mechanic, (or mechanician as such were termed), who saw another rocket. That there was a vessel in distress was quickly confirmed by the coast-guards at the Westward Ho! out-post. The lifeboat was immediately launched, at around quarter to ten, under the direction of her coxswain. As the lifeboat crossed the Bar, a member of the crew saw the rockets that were fired from the Down End coast-guards in order to guide the lifeboat to the stricken *Ceres*. The lifeboat reached the *Ceres* at a quarter passed eleven. The final matches were struck by the skipper to guide the lifeboat and her crew to the rowing boat.

What an amazing record of courage, endeavour and effort by all involved! Wreck and rescue has always been a part of the lives of the coastal communities. Such would always be a matter of news and record. But this wreck and rescue, involving as it did the one hundred and twenty-five-year-old *Ceres,* was not only reported locally, but also nationally and internationally. Her skipper and her mate, although they did have their photograph taken the next day outside St Mary's Church, Appledore, would not have been all that aware of this for a number of reasons. Walter's Certificate of Discharge can be seen to be dated for the day after the loss of the *Ceres,* that is, for 25th November 1936. The clothes they had been wearing when rescued that night would not have had time to dry. No recovery time, certainly no counselling in those days and, most significant of all, no job.

RESCUED CREW OF THE CERES

4. Oswald Jeffery and Walter Ford, outside St. Mary's Church,
Appledore, taken 25th November 1936

CERTIFICATE OF DISCHARGE.

FOR A SEAMAN NOT DISCHARGED BEFORE A SUPERINTENDENT OF A MERCANTILE MARINE OFFICE

ISSUED BY THE
BOARD OF TRADE
IN PURSUANCE OF
57 & 58 VIC., CH. 60.

Name of Ship and Official Number, Port of Registry and Tonnage.	Horse Power.	Description of Voyage or Employment.
Ceres Padstow 15560 32	36	Home Trade

Name of Seaman.	Year of Birth.	Place of Birth.
Walter Henry Ford	1708	Appledore

Rank or Rating.	Numbers of Certificates (if any).	
	Dis. A. No.	Any other Cert.
mate	—	—

Date of Engagement.	Place of Engagement.
15/7/30	Bude

Date of Discharge.	Place of Discharge.
25/11/36	Appledore Ship foundered

I Certify that the above particulars are correct and that the above-named
Seaman was discharged accordingly.

Dated this ..25.................. day of ..November..............197.36

Signature of
Master....A. G. Jeffery

Signature
of Seaman :

Signature of
Witness.....C. Thwick

W H Ford

Occupation ....Owner...........

Address ..38 The Strand Bude

NOTE.—Any person who forges or fraudulently alters any Certificate or Report, or copy of a Report, or who makes use of any Certificate or Report or copy of a Report which is forged or altered or does not belong to him shall for each such offence be deemed guilty of a misdemeanour and may be fined or imprisoned.

N.B.—Should this Certificate come into the possession of any person to whom it does not belong, it should be handed to the Superintendent of the nearest Mercantile Marine Office, or be transmitted to the Registrar General of Shipping and Seamen, Tower Hill, London, E.1.

Price 4d. per quire.

351 WL.28336/18606 75,000 4/25 JWL&O 183/10

5. Walter Ford's Certificate of Discharge, 25th November 1936

B

The *Ceres:*

i) Recollections and records

The *Ceres* was built in 1811 at Salcombe in South Devon. Her net registered tonnage, at that time, was thirty-two tons and she was able to carry fifty-four tons of cargo. Her construction was financed by a consortium of eight local businessmen and bankers, each of whom bought eight of her sixty-four shares. Originally the *Ceres* had been built as one of the heavily-rigged fruit smacks, which, fast for their size, plied their trade between Northern Spain and London. When first built her port of registry was Dartmouth. This transferred to Padstow in 1837. Her first captain was Captain William Lewis, a position he was to hold for the next eighteen years, until, on his death, the command of the *Ceres* was handed onto his eighteen-year-old son, also named William Lewis.

The *Ceres* was considered to be the fastest little vessel of her time. It comes as no surprise to learn, therefore, that she came to the notice of the British Government of the day during the final years of the Napoleonic Wars. The *Ceres* was commandeered for service as a fleet auxiliary. She carried military stores and other supplies to the Duke of Wellington's forces for the two years 1813 and 1814. The *Ceres* was fortunate in that she was both a new and strongly built vessel, sailed and cared for by men who knew not only how to sail such a vessel, but also how look after a wooden, sea-going sailing ship. It would be a further hundred years before her first auxiliary engine was fitted.

The second William Lewis, eighteen years old in 1829 when he took over the command of the *Ceres*, became, in the fullness of time, a grandfather. The grandson of this William Lewis wrote an article about the *Ceres* which was published, in 1929,

18

in the maritime magazine *Sea Breezes*. The following paragraph, a direct quote from his article, captures something of what it must have been like to sail to-and-fro across the English Channel during those final years of the Napoleonic Wars:

'My grandfather had many souvenirs from the *Ceres*, including the two old flintlock pistols which his father and the mate carried to shoot Napoleon and his bodyguard if they attempted to board the *Ceres*; the old horn lantern that was lighted by a tallow candle, made by the crew; the lantern, the only light, was carried at the bowsprit end when possible, to light the *Ceres* to glory; the old bull's horn which was used as a foghorn; also a piece of flint and steel used to strike a light with.'

Superb seamanship and care ensured that the *Ceres* not only survived those two turbulent years of her early life, but also avoided being captured by the French, a fate befalling a number of her sister ketches. The ketch *Good Intent* was one such but was also one that lived to trade another day. She was

6. The *Good Intent,* Bridgewater, probably 1890

built at Plymouth in 1790, registered at Bridgewater where, probably in 1890 on her hundredth anniversary, a photograph was taken of her.

Following her two years of war service the *Ceres* appears in the Supplement to Lloyd's List for 1815-1816. Such pages are awkward to read because the information recorded is sparse, cramped, smudged, peppered with abbreviations and subject to all the problems of classification and error. It was at that time still early years for the Lloyd's List. For instance, the category list for 1795 does not include the vessel type 'smack', so the *Ceres* begins to be identified as a 'sloop'. The *Ceres* can also be located in the 1817-1818 Lloyd's List. By this slightly later date the name 'Ceres' has become rather popular, for there are several pages of vessels named *Ceres* listed for these years.

One possible reason for the popularity of the name 'Ceres' may well have been astronomical. At the beginning of the nineteenth century telescopes became more powerful and asteroids were seen for the first time in the night skies. One large asteroid was named 'Ceres'. The name of this particular newly identified heavenly body would appear to have well and truly captured the imagination of the owner-captains of the day, if the number of vessels named 'Ceres' is anything to go by.

The *Ceres* is to be found on the fourth line up from the bottom of the 1815-1816 page, illustrated opposite. By 1817-1818 the names of the vessels are more organised, and in fact the number of vessels named 'Ceres' is so great that it is the owner-captains of the vessels who are are listed in alphabet order. Our *Ceres,* the subject of this small book, will be found on the tenth line up from the bottom of the 1817-1818 page. She remains identified as a 'sloop', but her shallow draught is correct as is her A1 condition. The classification A1 dates from these times. It is interesting to note that, at the time of

Ship		Master	Tons	Build	Date	Owner		Destination		
Cerberus S		M'Willm	370	Sndrl'd	1816	Lang&Co	17	Sd Grnld	A	1
			s D B							3
Chance Sr	A.C.	A. Reed	130	A.P.		Godfrey	11	PlLisbon	E	1
			& D			Sharp				3
Catherine Ali-	ce Bg	D. Oliver	114	British		Foreign	10	LoHavre	E	1
			a D							3
Clio	Sp	Wray	86	Whtby	1816	Barry	9	WyShlds	A	1
			& D							3
Channery S		Dowdale	358	N Imp	1815	Pott&Co.	17	Br N.Yrk	A	1
			s n P	P.Sds						4
Cashier Bg		Fales	204	Rd Isld	1811	Capt.&Co	13	Br N.Yrk	A	1
						A.				4
Catharine &	Ann Sp	H. Swart	32	Dutch		Foreign	6	Lo Amstr	E	1
			& n							4
Concordia Bg		Noray	215	Abrdn	1815	Mair	15	LoPhilad	A	1
			s D B							4
Charming Mol	l-ly Sp	Ferrier	63	Dover		Stewart	9	LoCoastr	B	1
			& n							4
Clio	S	Gardner	330	Massa.	1815	Richardsn	16	Li Boston	4	1
				O & Hk Mk P Sds						4
Castlereagh S J		Rowley	375	N.Brns	1815	Barlow	16	Li StJhns	A	1
			s D B	BB. Hk H & P						4
Cora S	& C lm.	Newcomb	386	Massa	1809	Richardsn	16	Li Savah		
				O.&P. 5PL.K				bad Repair		4
Choice Sw	s 15	Joicey	320	Shields	1801	S Hurry	15	ShLndon	E	1
			s D B	NKI s D	rp.05	ptNU W&I-p	15			4
Cacadore Sw		Rodriques	200	Plymh	1807	Thompsn	3	Lo NOrls	A	1
										4
Charles Bg		Janson	211	For'gn		Foreign	12	LoRtrdm	E	
			a D							4
C mm dore	Perry S	W Holmes	230	Amer.	1813	Arnold	15	LoSwedn	A	
										4
Canadian Pac-	ket Bg	Ballatine	230	Sndrl'd	1816	Booth&C	14	Sd Lndon	A	1
			s D B			Taylor		dA bad Rel		4
Cora S	& C lm.	Newcomb	336	Massa.		Richardsn	6	Li Savan		
						bad Repair A.				4
C untess of	Moreley S s.C.	H. Best	331	Kg's td	1801	Billing	16	Pl S.Seas	E	1
										5
Collingwood	Bg	T. Smith	120	Sndrl'd	1816	Capt.	11	LoCoastr	A	1
			s D B							5
Ceres Sp		J. Russell	57	Saltcb	1812	Capt.	7	LoCoastr	A	1
			s E							5
Cornwallis S	s.C.I.B.12	Charitte	720	Bengal	1812	Capt&Co.	20	Lo Bngal	A	1
			s Ds	Tea						5
Clasma Mar-	garetta Dr	Schapper	75	Hollnd	1815	Foreign	6	LoRtrdm	A	1
			a D							5
Christina Tiete	Dr	A. Potyen	101	Hollnd	1809	Foreign	9	Lo Antw	E	1
			& D							5

7. Supplement to Lloyd's List, 1815-1816

351	Ceres	Bg	Lincoln	197	Massa	1806	Miller & C	12	Lo Amer	E 1	
					pt *Sprce* P. P.		Sds A.			1812	
2	—	Sp	W. Ling	108	Dan.P.		Gardner	8	LoCoastr	E 1	
				s d						1811	
3	—	Dr	B. S. Low	101	Hollnd		Foreign	9	LoAmstr	E 1	
				s d						4	
4	—	S	T. Lunt	286	Amer.	1805	E. Brown	15	Li N.Yrk	A 2	
				s d	O.&P.P	TSds				1811	
5	—	S	T. Lyall	318	F.P.		Powell&C	15	Li Calcut	E 1	
	s.C.mstlyCB.15				ShrpDr	p.&lr	p.15			1816	
6	—	Sp	M'Inlay	70	Scotl'd	1790	Banatyne	9	Li Coast.	E 1	
				s d						1813	
7	—	Sw	G Mathew	250	Dndee	1814	Capt.	14	Lo Jamai	A 1	⋀
	s.C.14			s d d	11 PrI.S	&K.				11	
8	—	Sp	Marshall	82	Scotl'd	1802	Milne	9	Gr Baltic	E 1	
				s d	nBKl,T	Sds &	Drp.10			1815	
9	—	Bg	Mennell	150	Whtby	1793	Hodge	12	ShLondn	E 1	
				s d d	NKl Kl	sn&lr	p.15			1816	
360	—	Sp	WNewton	54	Scotl'd	1802	J. Milne	7	Hl Glsgo	A 1	
				s d						1811	
1	—	Bg	W. Owen	81	Brmth	1799	Capt&Co.	10	Li Coast.	E 1	
				s d	Srprs12					1814	
2	—	Bg	T. Pull	112	Yrmth	1803	Otty& Co.	10	YaCoast.	E 1	
				.d d	Srprs14					1816	
3	—	Bg	J. Poole	159	Whtvn	1812	Peil & Co.	12	LiLimrik	A 1	
			Hockdale	s d d						11	
4	—	Bg	Quindrell	265	Philad	1817	T. Eyre	14	BePhilad	A 1	
				s d d			A.			7	
5	—	Sw	J. Roose	133	Brmth	1796	Bibby&C.	11	LiDublin	E 1	
				s d d	pt nw.&	TSds	13,ptnD.14			1816	
6	—	Sp	J. Russell	57	Sltcmb	1812	Capt.	7	LoCoastr	A 1	
				s d						1816	
7	—	S	Rogers	279	N.Orls	1810	Scott	16	Li Amer.	A 2	
					P.P Sds					1812	
8	—	Bg	W Rowley	100	Dndee	1776	Langtry	10	LiBelfast	E 2	
		s		s d d	trp.03					9	
9	—	Bg	Schultz	192	Prusia		Roupel	12	Li Memel	E 1	
					Srprs 07					1814	
370	—	Sw	Schroder	225	Konin	1797	Goartret	14	Li Pillau	E 1	
				s d d						1814	
1	—	Bg	A Schraut	154	Swedn		Capt.	11	LoAmstr	E 1	
				s d	Ok &Fr					1814	
2	—	S	Seaward	276	Nby Pt	1808	Thorn	15	Li Amer.	A 1	
										1812	
3	—	Bg	J. Scott	112	Mntrse	1799	Capt.	10	Lo Hlgld	E 1	
				s d d	len05,D	rp.07				1814	
4	—	Bg	Stoffells	129	Prusia	1804	Foreign	9	Lo Lisbn	E 1	
				s d						1815	
375	—	Bg	Taylor	103	Blythe	1798	Bulmer	10	Lo Havre	E 1	
				s d d	Srprs 16	drp17				6	

8. Lloyd's List, 1817-1818

these nineteenth century lists, Salcombe still retained the 't' of the earlier spelling.

One of the remarks often made about the *Ceres* as she worked her way into the first decades of the twentieth century, was that she was the oldest vessel listed on Lloyd's Register. The postcard illustrated below was produced in 1934, and actually carries this piece of information at the base of the photograph. This observation remains one of those things always said of the *Ceres* now, although in actuality, particularly in the 1930s, this was a rather close run thing. There were several Scandinavian ketches built in the 1780s and 1790s that were still about and working in the 1930s. And, closer to home, there was the ketch *Jane,* built eleven years before the *Ceres* in 1800 at Runcorn. The *Jane* was registered, afloat and working, albeit as a stationary coal storage barge moored alongside a brewery at Bristol in the 1930s. She had been used as such since 1925 until she sank at her moorings in 1936. Realistically there can be no comparison between the two ketches, the *Ceres* and the *Jane*, but this date information about the *Jane* and the other vessels serves to illustrate the

9. Postcard of the *Ceres* at Bude, 1934

difficulties attached to definitions, categories, classifications and suchlike.

The *Ceres* appears only briefly in Lloyd's Register. Up until 1875, understandably, Lloyds only included those vessels that they had surveyed. After 1875 all vessels were included whether surveyed or not, but by then Lloyd's only listed the vessels that were over one hundred tons on their Register. The *Ceres* started off at thirty-two net registered tons and even after her enlargement was still well under the hundred, at forty-four net registered tons. However, between 1834 and 1875 Lloyd's Register did include all ships on the list.

LLOYD'S REGISTER

OF

BRITISH AND FOREIGN

SHIPPING.

From 1st JULY 1835 to the 30th JUNE 1836.

———

ESTABLISHED 1834.

LONDON:

PRINTED BY J. L. COX AND SONS, 75, GREAT QUEEN STREET, LINCOLN'S-INN FIELDS.

———

1835.

10. 1835 Lloyd's Register Title Page

C

No.	Ships.	Masters.	Tons.	BUILD. Where.	BUILD. When.	Owners.	Port belonging to.	Destined Voyage.	No. Years first assigned.	Character for Hull & Stores.
276	Celia	S C.35 / Davidson, J. Black	557	N Brns BB.& P.	1831	Harrison	Belfast	Liv.Quebec	4	A 1 b
7	—	J Grayson	159				Wthavn			
8	—	H'thrngtn	83				Padst'w			
9	—	Sr 1 B / J. Pearse	47	P'nznc lrp.34	1826	R Cornish	P'nznce	Pnz.Nwp'rt	10	A 1 34
280	Celt pt s.&C.32	Bg / A. Taylor	217	Grnck	1832	Muress&c J.Blair	Gr'nock	Cly.Venice	10	A 1 34
1	Ceneus	Swinburn	194				Sndrlnd			
2	Centurion Bg	J. Brand	186	Mntrse	1826	A. Brandt	M'ntrse	Dun.Ptrsbg		Æ 1 34
3	—	Hippenstl	468				Scarbro			
4	Cepheus	M'Intosh	105				Nwcastl			
5	Ceres	J Addison	322				London			
6	—	Bg C.33 / J. Adey	151	Brdprt	1817	Harrison	Poole	Lon.Nwflnd		Æ 1 34
7	—	Aldridge	89				Harwch			
8	—	W. Baker	52				London			
9	—	T. Barret	218				Sligo			
290	—	Sr / C. Bates	94	Gnsbro	1834	Furley&C	Hull	Liv.Coaster	10	A 1 34
1	—	J. Baynes	201				Nwcastl			
2	—	Blamfield	250				Jersey			
3	—	G. Brown	71				Gr'nock			
4	—	Bg / Craighead	143	Nwbrg pt ND.33	1826	W. Gill	Nwbrgh	Lon.	8	Æ 1 34
5	—	W. Fowls	113				Sndrlnd			
6	—	J. Grundy	106				Stocktn			
7	—	A. Harper	74				Gren'ck			
8	—	Sk / Hildreth	120	Brwck	1814	Wlson&C	Berwck	Bwk.Londn		Æ 1 34
9	—	Bk I.B. / C.Jobson	120	Wdbge len.ND.&lrp.33	1785	Capt&Co	Ipswich	Ips.		E 1 b
300	—	JKnowles	58				Drtmth			

11. 1835 Lloyd's Register entry for *Ceres,* bottom line

The 1835 Edition of Lloyd's Register of British and Foreign Shipping has an entry for the *Ceres*. Illustrations ten and eleven are of the title page of this particular edition and the page on which the *Ceres* information appears on the bottom-most line of print. Again, there remain a large number of other vessels named *Ceres*.

Once the Mercantile Navy List commenced publication in 1850 the *Ceres* disappeared forever from Lloyd's Register of Shipping. The *Ceres* information was transferred to the Mercantile, (or Merchant) Navy List where it remained to the end of her days, some eighty-six years later. Although correctly identified as a ketch in this entry, (she was ketch rigged in 1865), her recorded weight in 1936, remains at thirty-two tons. In 1868 she was lengthened by fifteen feet and her net registered tons at that time increased to forty-four tons.

Official No.	Name of Ship and Port of Registry	Rig.	Where and When Built.	International Code Signal (Visual).	Registered Tonnage	Owner, or Part Owner, and Manager (if recorded). × Signifies Managing Owner. Italics signify Manager.
103585	Cedric, Chatham, N.B.	Sr.	Caraquet, N.B. . 1896	..	14	Philip Rive, Caraquet, N.B.
104931	Cereal, Faversham	Spl.	Whitstable . 1894	..	43	Daniels Brothers (Whitstable), Lim., Sea Wall, Whitstable, Kent. *Harry K. Daniels, Kelvin House, Nelson Rd., Whitstable.*
109984	Ceres, London	—	Hull . 1898	..	116	W. H. J. Alexander, Lim., St. John's Wharf, Wapping, London, E.1. *William P. Alexander and George F. Alexander, same address.*
15560	Ceres, Padstow	K.	Salcombe . 1811	M.Q.G.C	32	× Alfred Petherick, Bude, Cornwall.
90988	Cerf, Rochester	Spl.	Frindsbury . 1886	..	44	Associated Portland Cement Manufacturers, Lim., Portland House, Tothill St., London, S.W.1. *James A. White, same address.*
163085	Cerigo, Dartmouth	Cr.	Fairlie . 1926	..	17	Dr. Thomas H. Ward, M.D., Weston House, Totnes, Devon.
98848	Cerise, Southampton	Cr.	Southampton . 1891	M.F.W.G	1	Philip H. Dodgson, Milford Grove, Salisbury, Wilts.
128340	Cessful, Townsville	K.	Thursday Is. . 1920	..	13	Charles E. Sinclair, Thursday Is.
114327	*Cetonia, Cowes	Sr.	Gosport . 1902	G.S.K.R	140	Rt. Hon. Hugh, Baron Stalbridge, Pounds Farm, Eastbury, Newbury, Berks.
115814	Cetus, London	Spl.	Grays . 1902	M.F.K.T	75	E. J. & W. Goldsmith, Lim., 110, Fenchurch St., London, E.C.3. *Edward J. Goldsmith, same address.*
150986	†Chack-Chack, Vancouver, B.C.	Yl.	Roberts Creek, 1923 B.C.	..	12	James N. Simmonds, 1031, Harwood St., Vancouver.
109223	‡Chad, Falmouth	Yl.	Wyvenhoe . 1900	M.F.F.M	3	× Cmdr. Edward A. Priestley, R.N.R., St. Chads, Montefiore Avenue, Ramsgate, Kent.
125019	Chaffinch, Fremantle, W.A.	Sr.	Fremantle, W.A. 1910	..	13	Herbert M. Parkes, Onslow, W.A.
155367	Chafi, Mombasa	—	Gainsborough . 1924	..	41	African Wharfage Co., Lim., Kilindini, Kenya Colony.
128422	Chaha, Ipswich	K.	I. of Wight . 1902	M.P.T.N	4	William G. Iliffe, Moorcroft, Farleigh, Whyteleaf, Surrey.
141506	Chaland 25, Quebec	—	Quebec . 1919	..	140	Northern Construction Co. & J. W. Stewart, Lim., 1010, St. Catherine St. W., Montreal, P.Q.
141507	Chaland 26, Quebec	—	Quebec . 1919	..	143	Northern Construction Co. & J. W. Stewart, Lim., 1010, St. Catherine St. W., Montreal, P.Q.
108935	Challenge, St. John's, N.F.L.	Sr.	Ship Cove, 1898 N.F.L. Rebuilt, New Port, Bona-vista Bay, N.F.L. 1922	..	50	James Baird, Lim., St. John's, N.F.L.
140007	Challenger, Lowestoft	Dy.	Oulton Broad . 1920	..	24	Leonard W. Head, 21, Tennyson Rd., Lowestoft. *William J. Head, same address.*
67096	Challenger, Rochester	Spl.	Rochester . 1875	M.J.J.W	43	Arthur Gamman, Lim., 14, St. Mary Axe, London. *Edwin Nicholson, Holborn Wharf, Chatham, Kent.*
135391	Chamois, Cowes	K.	Stonehouse . 1917	..	27	Crouchers, Lim., 6, Quay St., Newport, I. of W. *Percy J. Croucher, same address.*
10814	Champion, Bridgwater	K.	Bristol . 1853	..	68	× John W. Baker, 30, Worcester St., Gloucester.
29854	Champion, Ipswich	Spl.	Ipswich . 1861	M.C.Q.C	36	× Thomas Moore, 13, Beddome St., Walworth, London.
94130	Champion, Newcastle, N.S.W.	Cr.	Stockton, N.S.W. 1895	..	86	Peter Callen & Sons, Lim., Market St., Newcastle, N.S.W.
123443	Champion, St. John's, N.F.L.	Sr.	Petit Fort, 1905 N.F.L.	..	20	William C. Job, St. John's, N.F.L.
131726	Champion, R., Nassau, N.P.	Sr.	Hope Town, 1913 Abaco, Bahamas.	..	23	Chatham Albury, Harbour Island.
161971	Chan, Singapore	Lug.	Singapore . 1924	..	80	Ahna I. Sahib, 123, Teluk-Ayer Street, Singapore.
111351	Chance, Cape Town	K.	Brixham . 1900	Z.S.M.K	43	Stephan Brothers, Lim., 48, Bree St., Cape Town.
140052	Chanceport, St. John's, N.F.L.	Sr.	Burlington, 1916 N.F.L.	..	23	Sandy Knight, Morton's Harbour, N.F.L.
161837	Chancer, Leith	Lr.	Montrose . 1903	..	29	Andrew Robertson, 30, Craigentinny Crescent, Portobello, Edinburgh. *Thomas Robertson, same address.*
156741	‡Chandalar, Dawson, Y.T.	—	Winslow, Wash., 1905 U.S.A.	..	342	British Yukon Navigation Co., Lim., Vancouver, B.C.
139709	Chang Kiang, Shanghai	—	Shanghai . 1916	..	71	Asiatic Petroleum Co. (North China), Lim., St. Helen's Court, Great St. Helen's, London.
127160	Change, St. John's, N.F.L.	Sr.	Exploits Bay, 1909 N.F.L.	..	55	George Carter, Greenspond, N.F.L.
120191	Changli, Shanghai	Lr.	Shanghai . 1907	..	468	Taku Tug & Lighter Co., Lim., Hong Kong.
136547	Changtai, Singapore	Lug.	Singapore . 1916	..	119	Ho C. Chan, 261, Beach Rd., Singapore.
155368	Changu, Mombasa	—	Gainsborough . 1924	..	71	African Wharfage Co., Lim., Killindini, Kenya Colony.
148747	Chanticleer, London	Cr.	Gravesend . 1924	..	5	William H. Rickinson, 38, West Park Rd., Kew, Surrey.
154315	Chantier Maritime No. 1, Quebec	Scow.	St. Laurent, Is- 1926 land of Orleans.	..	155	Chantier Maritime de St. Laurent Limitee, St. Laurent, Island of Orleans, Que.
119004	Chantress, Fremantle, W.A.	Sr.	Fremantle. . 1903	..	12	Baden P. Wills, Darwin, N.T.

* Formerly the " L'Esperance." † Formerly the " Odanil." ‡ Formerly the " Verven."
‡ Foreign name " Beaver."

12. 1936 Mercantile Navy List entry for *Ceres*

13. Walter Ford with Fluff onboard the *Ceres* in 1936

ii) Episodes and experiences

The *Ceres* was forty-one years old when thirty-two of her sixty-four shares were bought by the Pethericks of Bude in 1852. The Pethericks were coal merchants, general and agricultural merchants, and, significantly for the *Ceres*, master mariners. Four generations of this family were destined to own, trade and sail the ketch *Ceres* for the rest of her one hundred and twenty-five years.

The *Ceres* would have been well-known in Bude by the time 1852 came round, for her first visit there had been in 1826 with a load of timber from Plymouth, following the successful completion of the inner harbour and sea locks at the sea end of the Bude Canal. The Bude Canal project was started in order to improve trade to the Port of Bude, to create a waterway for the transport of goods between Bude and Plymouth and to transport the lime rich coastal sand to improve the infertile soils of inland Devon and Cornwall. It had been a far-sighted and innovative project, but was never the business success all who had put up the money had hoped. Only thirty-five and a half miles of the sixty intended miles of canal were ever completed, and this included six inclined planes, the highest number for any canal in England.

The business of the canal never really got going. Dividends for the investors were at best minimal and for the most part, non-existent. The farmers could see no reason to pay for a load of sand when a boy and a cart could, for free, go down to the beach and bring sand back. Documents of the time indicate that the canal agent had money neither for taxes, dues, invoices or salaries. At one point the canal engineer's annual salary was cut by two-thirds to just over fifty pounds. The business of the canal was wound up at the turn of the century.

However the completion of the inner harbour and the sea locks at the sea end of the Bude Canal by 1823 could well have been the determining factor in the 1826 *Ceres* delivery of timber to Bude. Tucked away on a lee shore, Bude has never been the easiest of harbours. Access has always been complicated, requiring quite specific help to get into, and out from, the sea lock and the inner harbour. There were also a few days each month, even on a high tide, when access would not have been, and still is not, possible.

All vessels coming in to Bude had to wait until a flag, flown at Compass Point, indicated that the harbour could be entered. Vessels would then have to pass close to the breakwater and to both Barrel and Chapel Rocks. The hobblers, or hovellers, met each vessel off the end of the breakwater and, from their open rowing boat, would get a rope aboard the incoming vessel and align it to the harbour entrance using ropes and the warping posts, a procedure known as warping. There are those who recall today when, as youngsters, they 'helped' the hobblers. The speed and beauty of the incoming vessels is still remarked upon, as is the excitement when taken on board the incoming vessels. As an eight-year-old, Michael Haydon of Bude, can recall the *Ceres* coming in to Bude. The following is an extract taken from a taped interview with him:

'And when they were coming in we used to go down to the harbour and lock gates. Mr Pethick was the pilot... and they used to take four of us boys at a time. And once you'd been you didn't go (again), four others went next time.... Sometimes in the winter we had five minutes to get away. I used to go down. There used to be a little hut there called the hobble house, all the old ropes and that in there... they used to have a little bogy stove in the middle going and you used to sit on the ropes and listen to all the old sailors' yarns... And they used to pull us aboard, (the *Ceres*)... and we used to have the sail up, sail back... go nearly up to Lundy and back and then come in... yeh, it was great.'

14. The *Ceres* entering Bude with the hobblers

15. The *Ceres* at Bude, the Breakwater, Barrel and Chapel Rocks in the background

Ed Pethick, the Mr Pethick the pilot mentioned above, and some sixteen years older than his younger contemporary, recalls both the hobblers and the warping:

'…. because coming in on the left hand side there's the beach, isn't there and there's buoys there, well there used to be, they're gone now I think, and on the right hand side you've got posts. So they'd throw out, Pickard used to do it with the old hobble boat, skulling you see, they'd put the old ropes across the lines and keep the whole thing in the middle of the course, see. And they got little tiny motors… well, the *Ceres* used to have a little tiny motor…..'

Of the eighty-five vessel strandings recorded in and around Bude during the final forty years of the nineteenth century, (such record-keeping was very much improved at this point in time), forty-seven were very close into the harbour. The vessels involved were either entering or leaving Bude harbour, mostly entering. About one in five of the 325 crewmen of the wrecked ships were lost, drowned within sight of land.

Bude is the only haven for mile upon mile of the unforgiving, formidable and reef-fringed cliffs that run almost due south from Hartland. The prevailing westerlies are just as unforgiving and dangerous on this most perilous of lee shores. The *Ceres*' record for never having drowned a single crewman was, and still is, astounding. The following old couplet is based on firm and terrible fact:

'From Padstow Bar to Lundy Light
A watery grave by day or night'

However, there were two deaths on board the *Ceres*, though neither on the high seas. It is probable that the *Ceres* may well have only come up for sale following the first death, that of her second captain, the second William Lewis, in 1848. He was not quite forty years of age, and had twenty years of experience

32

as master of the *Ceres* to his credit. This William Lewis died following serious injury on board the *Ceres* sustained from the upsetting of the windlass in weighing anchor. The *Ceres* was in Clovelly roads at the time. The accident happened at about four in the morning on Sunday 5th March 1848. He died later the same day. His death would have been a serious loss to all concerned, and could well have been a factor in the sale of such a well built, highly manoeuvrable and shallow draught vessel. For the next four years, until bought by the Pethericks of Bude, she was captained by one Captain Knowles.

The second death was over fifty years later. On 5th July 1902 the death of seventeen-year-old George Close was reported in the local paper: 'Falling from the crosstree on board the ketch *Ceres*, owned by Mr W. W. Petherick, of Bude, while the vessel was in the locks on Saturday, George Close, aged 17, was so badly injured that he died on Sunday.'

It was W. W. Petherick, her captain for forty-two years, 1886 until he retired in 1928, who always said of the *Ceres* that he had weathered many storms and hurricanes in her, and that she was always there; and that every one who went in her considered her to be one of the best sea boats afloat. Over the years these storms and hurricanes were recalled and remembered locally within the ever popular medium of the ballad. These storms, the rescues and the tragedies, were also widely reported in the newspapers of the day.

Trade was essential to the economy of the day, and the ketches and other sailing ships, laid up for the winter from the preceding October, would have had to set out again in the following March or April. Sometimes March would be all right and sometimes not as far as the weather was concerned. In March 1891, more than twenty years before her first auxiliary engine was installed, the eighty-year-old *Ceres,* carrying a cargo of slate from Portmadoc to Plymouth, rounded

c

Land's End to reach Plymouth in a storm that prevented many other vessels from making any port at all, either then or ever. This storm was subsequently referred to, in records and histories, as the Great Storm of 1891. It was in this storm that the Bideford ketch *Francis Beddoe*, having sailed from Bideford for South Wales, ended up in St Ives Bay after failing to reach the mouth of the River Severn.

These storms and hurricanes produced blizzards of hail and snow as well as frighteningly freezing temperatures. The blizzard of the Great Storm of 1891, having raged for the two days of 9th and 10th of March, saw the freezing to death of one twelve-year-old cabin boy on board the Bude ketch *Ant*, caught out at sea. He was John Stapleton serving, as was usual practice then, as the young crew member on board the family ketch. The Swansea balladeer, F. N. Beer, wrote a fifteen couplet ballad for twelve-year-old John Stapleton a few weeks afterwards in the April of 1891. However kindly meant, the gloss put on such a terrible event as freezing to death in a snowstorm at sea is very strange to read nowadays. One can only hope that John Stapleton's mother was able to draw some comfort from such lines as:

*'Goodbye parents and friends all. I feel not now the cold and pain.
Hark I hear the Clarion call. Your loss will be my Heavenly gain.'*

This same balladeer also wrote a twelve stanza ballad for the Bude schooner *Agnes* lost with all hands off Longships in the same storm. The *Ant* herself survived to trade for a further four years, finally being lost following a collision in 1895 while delivering cement to the Isle of Wight.

Possibly the *Ceres'* closest call was during a particularly bad north-westerly storm in 1900. On November 7th 1900 the *Ceres* was caught by this severe storm in Bude Bay but managed to make Padstow a few miles further south. Because of the force of the gale, the *Ceres* worked out of

34

Bude Bay and ran for Padstow. She entered Padstow harbour safely but, with an ebb tide and an eddy wind, she had to let go both anchors when under the dangerous Steppet Point. The *Ceres* struck the rocks, but the crew were able to jump ashore. At low water they were able to get aboard again and that night she was towed to Padstow pier where she was repaired. This same force 10 north-westerly, on the same day, wrecked the 406 ton Italian barque *Concezione,* carrying pit-props from Nantes to Swansea, some three miles to the windward of Bude at Widemouth, but with all hands saved.

16. The Italian barque, *Concezione,* wrecked below Bude, 7th November 1900

The following month, on 28th December 1900, the 589 ton Austrian barque *Capricorno*, carrying coal from Swansea to the Adriatic, was not so fortunate. She drifted onto the rocks at Compass Point, at the end of Bude Breakwater, in another severe north-westerly. The Bude lifeboat brigade fired a total of eight rockets in all, but due to the force of the storm failed to get a line aboard. Out of fourteen crew of the *Capricorno* only two survived. One man had managed to use a failed breeches buoy line to reach the safety offered by those linked together and standing in the heavy seas to pull out whom they could. The second survivor was washed ashore by the seas. The following photograph shows just how close to shore the *Capricorno* was when she was lost, as well as the number of those on the rocks trying to get help to her stricken crew.

17. The Austrian barque *Capricorno,* wrecked off Bude Breakwater, 28ᵗʰ December 1900

iii) Trade and the times

In 1868, three years after she had been ketch-rigged, the *Ceres* was enlarged in order to increase her cargo carrying capacity by some thirty tons to eighty-five tons. Bude was thriving during those middle years of the nineteenth century, with a population of something over two thousand. The merchants, the owner-captains and ship-builders, the crewmen, the traders, the farmers, the general businesses and stores, the drapers, outfitters, a photographic firm, a bakery and so forth, contributed to the tough but viable economy of the time.

Lading inwards
Coal, Bristol Stone, Slate, Timber, Merchandise,
Limestone, Shafts for Bude Canal Company, Culm,
Iron, Porter, Salt, Tobacco, Earthenware, Furniture,
Sand for casting iron, Bricks, Grindstones, Cider,
Tallow, Herrings, Castings, Fish, Deal, Granite,
Bone ash, Guano, Superphosphates and phosphates,
Oats, Cement, Gravel, Chairs, Sleepers, Slag, Flour,
Crackstone and Pipes.
Lading Outwards
Mainly sand in ballast, but occasional cargoes of Grain, Bark,
Scrap Iron, Iron Ore, Timber, Potatoes, Malt, Corn,
Manganese, Bath Stone and Household Goods.

---

18. The Trade of the Port of Bude

The *Ceres* was fifty-seven years old at the time of her 1868 size increase, by which date she had been a Bude vessel for sixteen of those years. She was lengthened by fifteen feet at Stapleton's Shipyard at Bude. These additional feet were put into her amidships, which was unusual in that such additions to wooden vessels were more usually carried out forward or aft. One of the manoeuvres involved in this process required that someone hold a batten of the desired length as the two halves of the vessel were winched apart. The batten-holding individual would then indicate when the gap so produced was correct. Both an accurate eye and steady hand would certainly have been needed! Virtually identical, though more technologically sophisticated, enlargement procedures are carried out today on both ships and aircraft. These are known as 'jumboisations', and the increase in length in ships, at least, is matched by an increase in speed. For a complete description of how such work would have been undertaken on the *Ceres*, by hand and with no powered equipment, the reader is referred to *'West Country Coasting Ketches'* written by Basil Greenhill and W. J. Slade and published in 1974.

The Bude harbour records for 1860 show that there were 18,000 tons of inward cargo delivered that year to Bude. In the fullness of time 1860 would turn out to be the best year ever for trade. It was also the year that Bude recorded the highest number of vessels ever trading to the port, three hundred and one. The bulk of this trade was fuel, with nearly two thirds of the overall total being coal and about a tenth culm, this latter being the fuel used to fire the lime kilns. General goods, which would have included household commodities, accounted for a further significant proportion of the inward cargoes. General goods featured in the harbour records until the road and rail links became established when this section disappears. Fertilizers and soil improvers, such as guano, (from South America by way of Bristol) limestone, (from South Wales), and phosphates were substantial imports and these continued, in diminishing quantities and with changes within the category, until the sea-trade ended around the time of the Second World War. Building materials, timber, slates and brick are there in the harbour records, but disappear around the time of the First World War. Split stone and railway construction materials, this latter booming in the years 1876 to 1880, feature sporadically. As the agricultural practices changed the soil improvers, guano and then lime, were gradually replaced by slag, eighty tons of which were in the hold of the *Ceres* the night she foundered.

The *Ceres* was always very much part of all this whole trade activity.

In 1860 she would have been one of the annual total of three hundred and one vessels coming into the Port of Bude. She was still there in the 1927 harbour records, but only as one of twenty-six. It was with a load of timber that the *Ceres* first visited Bude in 1826, it was while carrying slate that she weathered the Great Storm of 1891 and it was with slag in the final days of November in 1936 that she foundered. Built to last, the *Ceres* more than fulfilled the work demanded of her.

It has been estimated that the *Ceres*, during her one hundred and twenty-five years of trade, transported 250,000 tons of every type of cargo, the bulk of which was inward into Bude. The trade of the Port of Bude was, for the greater part, inward trade. There was only ever minimal export from the port. Some of this small export trade would have been very much now and then, with some of it coming, quite legitimately, from the wreck salvage or unused construction materials. For a time, there had been exports of bark to Ireland for the leather trade. The warehouse for storing the bark, the Bark House is still there, to be found in the vicinity of what is now the Bude Stratton Museum. But the main export from Bude was sand in ballast for which there was a small but ready market, often at the next port-of-call. By custom and practice the sand in ballast trade was a perk for the masters of the vessels and not usually general cargo.

The following 1897 photograph of shipping moored at Bude was used in the 1936 calendar produced by the Pethericks for their employees and clients. One such employee was Walter Ford, the then mate of the *Ceres*, and, as 1936 turned out to be the *Ceres'* final year, the calendar became a family keepsake. This 1936 calendar, as well as the identities of the moored vessels, also carries the explanation as to why the firm had decided to use what was, after all, a forty-year-old photograph: it was just more cheerful to have a picture of a thriving port rather than an empty one.

19. Shipping moored at Bude in 1897.

W. W. PETHERICK & SONS,
MERCHANTS,
BUDE.

Bude,
Dec., 1935.

Dear Sir or Madam,

It gives us much pleasure to send you our Calendar for 1936. The photograph belongs to the time when Bude was a real Port and was taken by J. Thorn in February, 1897.

The names of the Ships and their Captains are as follows :-

On the Left.		On the Right.	
1 Elizabeth	Capt. W. Brinton	1 Friendship	Capt. A. Stephens
2 Sir T. D. Acland	Capt. G. Hallett	2 Ant	Capt. H. Hines
3 Purveyor	Capt. H. Rooke	3 Brackley	Capt. Morgan
4 Tavy	Capt. H. Mountjoy	4 Joseph & Thomas	Capt. B. Shazell
5 Hawk	Capt. F. Martin	5 Stucley	Capt. W. Cook
6 Lady Acland	Capt. E. Cunningham	6 Wild Pidgeon	Capt. G. Barrett
7 Boconnoc	Capt. W. Sluggett	7 Ceres	Capt. R. W. Petherick
8 Kindly Light	Capt. J. B. Cook	8 Du I Win	Capt. J. Chidgey

Wishing you a Merry Christmas and a Prosperous New Year.

Yours faithfully,

W. W. Petherick & Sons.

(A. Petherick.)

20. The names of the vessels moored in the 1897 photograph

41

The Bude harbour records for the years between 1860 and 1927 reveal a steady, gradual decline in trade over those sixty-seven years. Well over three quarters of a million tons of cargo were brought into Bude during this time. It is understandable, though sad, that the busy port photograph of the 'good old days' would be more cheering than a 1936 scene of empty wharves. And, as can be seen from her Cargo Book for 1927/1935, the *Ceres* was still working, and working well, during these last years of hers, shipping in her maximum cargoes of eighty tons of the heavy weighing slag and fifty tons of the higher volume flour on a very regular basis.

The page recording her 1932 trade, illustrated on the following page, and from her 1927/1935 Cargo Book indicates that the timetable of slag brought from Port Talbot and flour or grain from Cardiff continued throughout the last years of the *Ceres*. Both commodities were transported in extremely fine weave bags, for both were like fine dust. Old friends of mine, farm children of the nineteen-thirties, can recall the slag being used, for they were kept indoors while it was being spread over the land. The men, the horses and the carts all had to be washed clean of the slag, for it billowed everywhere like smoke and got into everything.

The number of ships coming into Bude decreased and with it the overall tonnage shipped in. However, the vessels using Bude had to be below a certain size because of the difficult harbour and so the average cargo tons carried by each vessel remained relatively constant over the years. But the seeds of overall economic decline had been sown. The financial returns for those working out of Bude in their wooden vessels would only ever have been modest, three and four shillings a ton is mentioned, and sometimes not even that. Making a living was tough but possible. The last Petherick owner-captain of the *Ceres* estimated that, in the eighty-four years the *Ceres* had been owned by his family that she had brought into Bude £42,000 worth of freight, a substantial and valuable amount of business for the firm and the community.

Date Received.	Marks.	Number.	Description.	Solid Contents or Weight	Where Stowed.	Shippers.	Consignees.	Date Delivered.
July 5			Sailed from Appledore Light for Avonmouth				arr	5th
9th			Sailed from Avonmouth 80	tons Maize Bude			arr	11th
12th			Sailed from Bude Light	for Cardiff			arr	13th
14th			Sailed from Cardiff 40 tons	flour Cardiff & Channell mills Bude			arr	15th
19th			Sailed from Bude Light Port Tallot				arr	19th
20th			Sailed from Port Talbot	80 tons Basic Slag Bude arr				21st
22nd			Sailed from Bude Light for	Port Talbot			arr	22nd
29nd			Sailed from Port Talbot 80	tons Basic Slag Bude arr			Aug	2nd
Aug 1st			Sailed from Bude Light for	Avonmouth			arr	4th
7th			Sailed from Avonmouth 80	tons Maize Bude			arr	8th
9th			Sailed from Bude Light	for Cardiff			arr	10th
10th			Sailed from Cardiff 50 Flour	Cardiff & Channell mills Bude			arr	11th
12th			Sailed from Bude Light for	Avonmouth			arr	13th
14th			Sailed from Avonmouth 80 tons	Maize Bude			arr	15th
17th			Sailed from Bude Light for	Port Talbot			arr	17th
18th			Sailed from Port Talbot 80 tons	Basic Slag Bude			arr	19th
29			Sailed from Bude Light Lydney	arr				30th
31st			Sailed from Lydney 48 tons Dean Forrest House Coal Bude					16th

21. *Ceres* Cargo Book page for October 1932

Real fortunes were to be made in shipping during the nineteenth century, though not by vessels the size of the *Ceres*. The import of the fertilizer guano from South America is a case in point. There is at least one Victorian Gothic mansion, open to the public today, to the south-west of Bristol, that owes its being to the massive fortune made by one entrepreneur of the day who shipped in the guano from South America to Bristol for sale and onward distribution. Even so, this individual only just managed to make his fortune before the times changed and the guano trade ceased.

One recent study examining possible reasons for the total decline in the trade to the Port of Bude suggests that both the severe agricultural depression at the end of the nineteenth century and the First World War were far more influential than either the coming of the government subsidised railway to Holsworthy and Bude, at the beginning of the twentieth century, or the failure as a business of the Bude Canal, for which there never appeared to have been a meaningful business plan. The trade diminished, the ketches aged, disappeared and were not replaced. It would have made little economic sense to repair or replace vessels no longer required to transport cargo. Stapleton's Shipyard at Bude wound up its eighty-seven-year-old family-run business in 1917.

Even so, the *Ceres* had had the first of her auxiliary semi-diesel Swedish engines fitted in 1912, 20th July of the following year seeing her first motor voyage. This 30hp engine ensured her survival during the First World War, for this, combined with her shallow draught allowed the *Ceres* to keep close into shore and so escape the attentions of the enemy submarines. A number of ketches, more often than not used as decoys to sail over the coastal defence minefields, were blown out of the water by enemy submarines. Sometimes the crews were allowed into the ships' rowing boats before the ketch was torpedoed and sometimes not. The *Ceres'* engine also enabled her to assist fellow ketches in difficulties. The following picture shows the *Ceres* towing the *Francis Beddoe* out of Bude.

22. The *Ceres* with the *Francis Beddoe* in tow, Bude, July 1919

Her second engine, a Swedish semi-diesel again, was fitted in 1930. Oswald Jeffery mentions the quality of this engine when interviewed following the loss of the *Ceres*. The *Ceres'* cargo book records that the *Ceres* did not leave Hinks' Shipyard at Appledore in 1930 until the late May of that year. This would have been the time of the fitting of the new engine. Otherwise the *Ceres* was always back in business mid-April, at the start of the short six month trading year. The next photograph was specially taken at Appledore for the *Sunday Times* by the photographer J. Dixon-Scott in the 1930s.

Appledore, at the mouth of the River Torridge, is noted to-day, as in the past, for its shipbuilding. It is at the present experiencing a local boom, and every yard is busier than for many years past. The village has a history exceeding 1,000 years, and is mentioned in the Saxon Chronicle as the site of a great conflict between the Danes and the English in the ninth century.

23. The *Ceres* and other shipping, Hinks' Middle Yard, Appledore, 1930s

The vessels in the picture above are, from left to right, the *Penryn,* the *Ceres,* a fishing vessel belonging to Walter Ford's family, ribs only of the *Devon* and a longboat, the *Dabchick.* In the background on the further bank, are two of the laid up cargo ships. They were laid up there because the economy in general during the 1930s was not in good shape.

During the years of declining trade and fewer and fewer ketches, the *Ceres* came to play a more and more significant role in what was left of the trade into Bude. Articles about aspects of the *Ceres'* life and times started to appear in both the press and specialist maritime magazines, marvelling at her longevity, her time on Lloyd's Register and her good name among the maritime community. There also appeared, during the late twenties and early thirties, a few articles that challenged her claim to be the oldest vessel still working. But she was famous. Literally hundreds of photographs must have been taken of her, judging by the number of those that still survive. There is even one photograph of the key people in her life at the time waiting for her return to Bude.

24. Waiting for the *Ceres* to return, Bude, 1935/1936

Those in this picture are, from left to right:-

W. C. Edwards, J. T. Found, the then Bude harbour master, Captain W. W. Petherick, the recently retired master of the *Ceres*, Alfred Petherick, with binoculars, the then master-owner of the *Ceres*, 'Greener' Marshall, and J. Darch.

In 1929 an article was published that celebrated the amazing 1927 record for the *Ceres*, one that has never been bettered, while in charge of Captain W. W. Petherick, forty years her captain and well into his eighties at the time. A record three voyages were completed successfully between Saturday 8th October and Sunday 16th October, two to Port Talbot for slag and one to Cardiff for flour. The *Ceres* achieved the final passage, dock to dock, Cardiff to Bude, in just one tide. The year 1927 saw just over 2,000 tons of cargo brought into the Port of Bude. In this one October week the *Ceres* contributed about one tenth of that overall total.

October 1927
Saturday 8th: Arr. Bude. Dis. Cargo. Sailed for Port Talbot.
Sunday 9th: Arr.Port Talbot.
Monday 10th: Loaded slag. Sailed for Bude.
Tuesday 11th: Arr. Bude. Dis.Cargo. Sailed for Port Talbot.
Wednesday 12th: Arr. Port Talbot. Loaded slag. Sailed for Bude.
Thursday 13th: Arr. Bude. Dis.Cargo. Sailed for Cardiff.
October 14th: Friday: Arr. Cardiff on the evening tide
having had strong wind against her.
Saturday 15th: Loaded flour. Sailed for Bude.
Sunday 16th: Arr.Bude, having made this passage
from dock to dock in one tide.

---

25. The *Ceres* unbeaten record achieved in October 1927

For Customs Stamp, Port, and Date.

15

C E R E S ....(Use Block Capitals)

istry .... *Padstow*

.... *15560*

n .... *Home Trade*

.... via ....

gent ....

ERTIFY that Messrs. *W. W. Petherick & Sons*

um of .... *Two* .... Pounds, ... *five* .... Shillings,

.... pence in respect of LIGHT DUES for the above Voyage.

Signature of Collector .... *S. Roberts*

(a) STEAM or SAILING VESSEL.		£.	s.	d.
Home Trade. *1½*	Foreign Going.			
per Ton				
Net Register Tonnage *32 × 10*		2	5	0
Deck Cargo				
Add *12½ %* per cent. in accordance with Order in Council				
	£	2	5	0

PAYMENTS FOR CURRENT FINANCIAL YEAR (1935-36).

No. of Home Trade Voyages	*10*	
No. of Foreign Going Voyages	—	
Total Rate per ton paid to this date	*1/3*	
No. of Home Trade Payments during present month ...	*10*	

To include present payment.

I for Voyage next prior to that in respect of which Dues are now paid.

..........) at *Annual Payment 10 Voyages* .... 193....

r or Agent on paying the | (a) Strike out word which does not apply.
requested, for his own |

26. *Ceres* Light Certificate for 1935 – 1936

It has been estimated that, in her lifetime, the *Ceres* transported a quarter of a million tons of cargo. This being the case the existing documents suggest that the *Ceres* would have brought into Bude at least one third of the overall cargo of the Port of Bude between the year 1852, when she was purchased, and the year 1936, when she foundered.

No failures were allowed. The one time that the *Ceres* failed to deliver the goods due to bad weather there was quite a row. In fact a protest was held about it before Commander Thomas Craven at Bude. This was on 9th August 1911. The *Ceres* had left Cardiff for Bude with flour and bran for W. W. Petherick and Sons, the family firm, on 3rd August and had to put into Mumbles because of bad weather on 4th August. The *Ceres* left Mumbles some days later, on 8th August. She arrived at Bude that same evening at 9.00 p.m. On entering Bude Harbour at high water 6.00 a.m. the following morning, the *Ceres* struck the Bar owing to the ground swell, with some damage. There was uproar all round, though there was nothing that unusual about even the *Ceres* hitting things in and around Bude. There is one recorded instance when, while carrying coal inwards to Bude in 1893, she 'wrecked' on Summerleaze Cliff, and another while leaving Bude in ballast in 1899 she 'wrecked' on the rocks on the west side of the harbour.

The Bude harbour master in the twenties and thirties, J. T. Found, was the third generation of his family to hold the post. In 1935 he was interviewed for a feature article about the *Ceres* published in the national press and penned in the heroic language of the day. The article was headlined 'Old Faithful of Dead Port; 124-year ship still sails'. By 1935 the *Ceres* had become the last of the sea-going trading vessels to come into Bude. The photograph accompanying the article shows the *Ceres* alone, her rowing boat tied up alongside, and waiting for the tide.

A popular little trip for visitors to the town, and others at holiday

OLD FAITHFUL OF DEAD PORT

124-Year Ship Still Sails

From Our Special Correspondent

BUDE, Tuesday.

A SOLITARY mast showing black and distinct above a sea of grey slate house-tops guided my steps to the harbour.

This, I think, must be the smallest port of the West.

Here are no rattling winches and whistling tug-boats, no bales of costly cargo and gangs of sweating labourers.

Bude harbour is empty, deserted, its trade killed by the advent of the railway and modern methods of transportation.

SMALL PORTS OF THE WEST—7 A broad canal, a haven now for wild duck and gulls, capacious quays, rusting bollards and empty warehouses . . . signs of past industry almost forgotten . . . signs of times Bude will never see again.

At least, that was the opinion of Captain Cook. For close on seventy years he sailed from Bude.

HAD ITS DAY

Now he has retired, and although he goes day by day down to the harbour where once he brought his ships with their ever-changing cargoes, he believes that Bude has had its day.

But the fact that Bude can boast no imposing display of tonnage figures does not detract from its interest.

Let me tell you about the Ceres, the oldest vessel on Lloyd's register, the ketch which is Bude's only seagoing visitor.

She is the Grand Old Lady of the Merchant Service. It was her lonely

The solitary Ceres, last of Bude's sailing ships and (inset), Mr. J. T. Found, third of his family to be harbourmaster

flag-tipped mast which guided me to the quayside. . . .

" **Born 1811, and still going strong,**" is what folk say of the **Ceres. At the moment she is still laid up for the winter, safe from the fury of the winds and seas which make this coast so dangerous for shipping.**

In the galley I found the captain's wife. " Everyone in Bude is very proud of the Ceres," she told me. "All the visitors here make a special point of coming to see the boat."

ESCAPED PIRATES

In the early days the Ceres was a regular trader with ports on the coasts of Northern Spain. During that time she had many narrow escapes from roaming French and American privateers.

In 1813-14, when Wellington was pursuing his Peninsular War campaign, the gallant Ceres was employed by the Government to carry militar. stores to the scene of the fighting.

It was in 1826 that Bude flung wide her lock gates to receive the Ceres. In

West of England Edition

1852 she became the property of the Petherick family—merchants in Bude —and to this day she has not changed hands.

But to the man who is the third member of his family to hold the post of harbour master—Mr. J. T. Found—the old Ceres has come to mean something more than the oldest boat . . . she is the only boat.

Since 1854 a Found has been harbour master at Bude. The rosy-cheeked, happy man who told me of the port's decline has held his position for 23 years.

GRAVEL AND SLAG . . .

Last year there were 22 entries in Mr. Found's log-book . . . they showed the number of times the Ceres had returned home after voyaging to South Wales with gravel and slag.

" There was a time," Mr. Found told me, " when a regular service of coasting vessels was run from Bude to Bristol and other large ports. Most of the supplies of food for the town came from Bristol.

" Up to 1864, when the trade of Bude was at its peak, there were more than 50 vessels owned by merchants in the town "

Someone once made a record of Bude wrecks. The list, I am certain, has done nothing to assist the port in its fight for existence. From 1862 to 1900 86 vessels went aground here . . .

27. 1935 newspaper feature article about the *Ceres*

51

times, was always the short voyage by ketch from the locks as far as the bridge. This 1936 August Bank Holiday photograph of the *Ceres* decked out in bunting would be just such an occasion, with everyone out and about enjoying both the day and the little boat trip while raising funds for the lifeboats.

28. The *Ceres*, August Bank Holiday 1936

iv) Her ballad, legends and legacies

The Ketch 'Ceres'
1811-1936
'Without drowning a single crewman'

A century and a quarter of change and change had passed
Since they built her down in Devon, where they mostly build to last,
And sent her but to earn her keep, at risk of wind and war,
And dodge the nimble privateer along the Biscay shore.

And war went out, and peace came in, and time it went and came,
And brought new changes every year, but her it brought the same
And privateers they vanished, and the Indiamen likewise
And the first steam kettle trailed her smoke across the affronted skies.

The tea fleet and the wool fleet, in turn they had their day,
She marked them in their beauty as she plied upon her way,
Their canvas piled like summer clouds...like summer clouds they passed,
But she was built in Devon – and they build 'em there to last.

She knew the rips and overfalls from London to the Lizard,
And once she nearly left her bones off Padstow in a blizzard,
And when the winter fogs were thickest she mostly smelt her way
By the old familiar sea marks into Bude and Watchet Bay.

And peace went out and war came in, and forth she went once more,
To dodge the nimble submarines along the English shore,
And war went out and peace came in, and still she held together,
Spite of floating mine and tinfish and the good old English weather.

She loaded salt and timber, and she carried slate from Wales,
Cement and corn and cattle cake and paving stones and nails,
She worked her way to Liverpool and down the coast for cloam,
Across the way to Swansea Bay and then with slag for home.

But a time it comes to ships and men, when sailing days are passed
Even such as hail from Devon, where they mostly build to last,
And her seams began to open and the Severn tide came through,
And the water kept on gaining spite of all that they could do.

They did their best to beach her, but they couldn't do no more,
And they foundered at the finish in sight of Appledore,
And her bones'll never flicker blue on any longshore fire,
For she'll lie there and she'll moulder as any old ship might desire,
And hear the vessels passing by, and dream about the past,
And the great old times in Devon, where they built her once to last.

Towards the end of this ballad there is the line, 'And her seams began to open and the Severn tide came through'. There is only one other statement as to why the *Ceres* foundered and those are Walter's own words. Walter always said, within his family circle, that a recently replaced garboard plank had been of unseasoned timber and it was this that caused the *Ceres* to founder. The garboard planks are those next to the keel, right under the bow at the front of the boat. Eighty tons of bagged slag were stacked on top of this newly replaced plank that night. Pressure would have built up in the new wood, as the wood expanded with the sea water. This pressure would cause the seams between the new plank and the adjacent planks to open. In such a position, the water coming in would be concealed until the situation was beyond saving. This would have been what happened that night. The plank replacement must have been general knowledge for the balladeer to be aware of how the *Ceres* had come to founder, even though there would appear to be no other reference as to cause, apart from Walter's words.

The *Ceres* Commemorative Ballad was written by C. Fox Smith in February 1937 and was presented in a folded, cream-coloured quality card. The photograph of her coming into Bude with the hobblers was on the front cover. A large number of the commemorative cards were produced. The *Ceres*, by the time of her loss, had come to mean a great deal to the townspeople of Bude. It was, of course, the Ford family's card that was known to me and which Ann, Walter's daughter, has now given to Bude-Stratton Museum with her other *Ceres* memorabilia. The factual accuracy of the ballad-form was a crucial element of ballad making, particularly significant at times when the only meaningful method of communication between and within communities remained the spoken word.

This short exploration of the life and times of the *Ceres* has discovered that the two matters that contributed to her legendary fame, that of being the oldest vessel on Lloyd's Register and of never having drowned a single crewman, hold as true today as they have always done, though both rather close run things. The stuff of legends, the backbone and accuracy of oral histories and ballads, should never be discounted for such will always be the bedrock of history.

However, what the *Ceres* balladeer would not have known in 1937 was that, had the *Ceres* survived, in all probability she would have been commandeered by the wartime government of the 1940s, in order to form part of the balloon barrage defence at Falmouth, and eventually to rot away with the other ketches so taken. It is far, far better to look out to sea from the coast of North Devon between Down End and Bull Point Lighthouse and to know that the *Ceres* rests somewhere out there. The *Ceres* was indeed born under a fortunate star.

The very last that was ever seen of the one hundred and twenty-five-year-old ketch *Ceres* was the morning after she had

29. The *Ceres* on her visit last to Bude, November 1936

foundered, when just the top of her mast remained above the sea, visible from Down End and Bull Point. In such a position the *Ceres* presented a major hazard to coastal shipping. Without more ado, the *Ceres* was handed over to Trinity House who blew her up.

One question remains unanswered. There is nothing in the exploration of this short history of the life and times of the *Ceres*, that explains why was she out and about, carrying on her trade, at the end of November in 1936. Her Cargo Book records that the very latest voyage during her last eight years 1927 to 1935 was, on one occasion only in November, and that early in the month, on 2nd November. Every other year, the *Ceres* was laid up for the winter by the first week of October. There must have been talk about this late November voyage in 1936, for such was not usual practice. In all probability it came about because of an ill-judged business decision by a hard-pressed owner. Fortunately, two good Appledore crewmen lived to tell the tale. The legend of the *Ceres* held true to her very end.

30. The *Ceres* just visible on the skyline, heading for South Wales, September 1936

The *Ceres*:

i) Her Obituaries

The loss of the *Ceres* in 1936 attracted a remarkable degree of news coverage. The *Western Morning News and Daily Gazette* of 26th November 1936 carried the first of the reports of her loss, including a photograph of the skipper and the mate outside Appledore Church, and the word for word account of their rescue reproduced in an earlier section of this small book.

The *Cornish and Devon Post* also carried a full report of the loss of the *Ceres* on 28th November 1936, which was a Saturday. This is an account of the loss of the *Ceres* told very much for people of Bude and Cornwall. The actual date of her first arrival at Bude, 23rd June 1826, is mentioned here, as are the dates of her two long serving Petherick captains. The first of these was Captain W. M. Petherick who sailed the *Ceres* from 1868 to 1884. The second was Captain W. W. Petherick who sailed the *Ceres* from 1884 until he retired from the sea in March 1929. W. W. Petherick was the uncle of the last Petherick owner-captain of the *Ceres*, Alfred, more usually known as Alfie.

The *Cornish and Devon Post* news coverage of the loss of the *Ceres* also included the pleasure all had had, not only in seeing her into the locks at Bude, but also in travelling on board her the short journey along the canal to the road bridge. It is recorded in this report that a local lady, Miss O. Wharry of Whetstone, had on view at the 91st annual exhibition of the Royal West of England Academy at Bristol, a splendid sketch of the *Ceres*.

Both Walter Ford, the mate of the *Ceres* and the skipper that night, Oswald Jeffery, were Appledore men, Walter living in Irsha

FATE OF THE CERES

125-Years-Old Ketch Founders

DRAMA OFF NORTH DEVON COAST

Appledore Life-Boat Rescue

THERE was no sign yesterday of the Ceres, the Bude auxiliary ketch, oldest boat on Lloyd's Register, which, as briefly reported in yesterday's "Western Morning News," was abandoned by her crew of two late on Tuesday night, when the vessel was in a sinking condition off the North Devon coast.

The captain and mate, who were the only people on board, were rescued by the Appledore life-boat. The Ceres is believed to have foundered somewhere between Down End (Croyde) and Baggy Point.

The captain is Mr. Oswald Jeffery, a married man, whose home is at Richmond-road, Appledore, and the mate Mr. Walter Ford, a married man, of Irsha-street, Appledore.

They reached Appledore in the life-boat about eleven o'clock on Tuesday night, and on their arrival the Vicar (Rev. H. C. A. S. Muller) offered a short prayer of thanksgiving for their safety. He welcomed the men in his capacity as agent of the Shipwrecked Mariners' Society.

DANGER OF FOG

Too Rough To Proceed To Bude

The story of the ill-fated voyage is best told in the words of Capt. Jeffery, who said: "We left Swansea on Tuesday bound for Bude with a cargo of slag. There was a certain amount of fog, but we were successful in making Bull Lighthouse, and came past Morte Point into Morte Bay, intending to go in over the Bar for the night, as it was [...] —ugh to venture on to Bude, and a

31. Lead paragraphs, *Western Morning News and Daily Gazette*, 26th November 1936

CERES TO SAIL NO MORE.

125-YEARS-OLD KETCH FOUNDERS.

Sentimental Ownership of Bude Residents.

For some years the auxiliary ketch Ceres, of Bude, has been the oldest vessel on Lloyd's register. It is certainly the oldest vessel in service in the British Isles, and is believed to be the oldest vessel in the world. But now her long career of service has terminated for the Ceres was abandoned, Tuesday night, in the Bristol Channel in dense fog, after developing a leak. The leak occurred off Croyde, and as the water gained on the pumps rockets were fired at about 10 p.m., and were observed by the coast-guard at Down End.

The Appledore life-boat was speedily launched and the crew of two, Mr. Oswald Jeffery, the captain, who is resident of Appledore, and Mr. Walter Ford were taken ashore. Unfortunately they lost all their belongings but were taken to Appledore and looked after by Rev. H. C. A. S. Muller, the Vicar, who is a representative of the Shipwrecked Mariners' Society. They reached Appledore in the life-boat about eleven o'clock on Tuesday night, and on their arrival the Vicar (Rev. H. C. A. S. Muller) offered a short prayer of thanks-giving for their safety.

WATER IN ENGINE ROOM.

Describing the ill-fated voyage, Capt. Jeffery said they left Swansea on Tuesday bound for Bude with a cargo of slag. There was a certain amount of fog, but they were successful in making Bull Lighthouse, and came past Morte Point into Morte Bay, intending to go over the Bar for the night, as it was too rough to venture on to Bude, and a certain amount of fog added to the difficulty. At 8 o'clock he went below to rest for an hour, leaving the mate in charge. An hour later he came to Capt. Jeffery and told him there was water in the engine room. Capt. Jeffery rushed to the engine room and found the water being splashed about by the couplings of the engine. As he entered the room he found the water almost up to his waist. He went on deck and immediately manned the pumps and continued until he was overtaken by exhaustion. The mate took over and on returning to the engine room, Capt. Jeffery found that water was still rising. They tried to get the ship in over the Bar, but the volume of water made her roll badly and he gave orders for the ship's rowing boat to be launched.

FIRED ROCKETS.

In order to attract the attention of coastguards at Down End, he started firing rockets. He succeeded in firing two rockets but then the ship began to lurch so badly that he found it impossible to light any more with matches. He had to use flares, which is a risky procedure as the rockets are liable to explode at once. One exploded a few yards up in the air. He retained one rocket for the ship's boat and when the water was washing the decks of the Ceres, taking with them the ship's and other important papers, they abandoned the vessel. When in the ship's boat Capt. Jeffery fixed one rocket between

32 Lead paragraphs, *Cornish and Devon Post*, 28th November 1936

Street at the time, and Oswald Jeffery in Richmond Road. Both were young married men. The report in the *Bideford Weekly Gazette* was in all essentials, apart from the introductory paragraph and headline, the same as that of the *Western Morning News and Daily Gazette*. This first paragraph is written for the people of Appledore, and the names of the Appledore vicar and doctor as well as the identity of the Appledore lifeboat are prominent here, all elements of intense interest to those living in the immediate locality.

The Times for 4th December 1936 carried a superb account of the loss of the *Ceres* for the national readership. This report was a condensed history of the life and times of the *Ceres*, which included a glance at the Napoleonic Wars and some of the storms and hurricanes she had survived. *The Times* also printed a picture of her at Bude.

And, in Canada, there was a report of her loss, sent in by the London correspondent of the *Toronto Evening Telegram,* which was published in that paper on 12th December 1936. Walter's sister-in-law was living in Canada when the *Ceres* foundered. This lady had, with great care, cut out the relevant paragraph only and sent this back to the family in Appledore. From this tiny, seventy-year-old cutting, no date, no newspaper title, the Intellisearch facility of the Toronto Reference Library found both the paragraph and the page on which it appeared. Sharing the news on this page was a full report of the Abdication of Edward VIII as well as an account of an early dispute between the firms supplying syrup to the newly born Dionne quintuplets.

The *Ceres* passed into history after the completion of a remarkable one hundred and twenty-five year history of her own. There are at least five reports of her passing, her obituaries: few of us reading about the *Ceres* to-day will have more than one.

FATE OF THE "CERES."

125 YEARS-OLD KETCH

FOUNDERS OFF BAGGY.

SKIPPER'S GRAPHIC STORY.

THE 125-years-old "Ceres," veteran of the merchant service, her course now run, lies at the bottom of Bideford Bay, somewhere off Baggy Point.

The "Ceres" sprang a leak on Tuesday night, while on a voyage from South Wales to Bude and foundered after her crew had put off in her boat and had been picked up by the Appledore lifeboat.

The captain is Mr. Oswald Jeffery, a married man, whose home is at Richmond-road, Appledore, and the mate Mr. Walter Ford a married man, of Irsha-street, Appledore.

They reached Appledore in the lifeboat about eleven o'clock on Tuesday night, and on their arrival the Vicar (Rev. H. C. A. S. Muller) offered a short prayer of thanksgiving for their safety. He welcomed the men in his capacity as agent of the Shipwrecked Mariners' Society.

Rough Sea and Fog Danger.

The story of the ill-fated voyage is thus told by Capt. Jeffery :—

"We left Swansea on Tuesday bound for Bude with a cargo of slag. There was a certain amount of fog, but we were successful in making Bull Lighthouse, and came past Morte Point into Morte Bay, intending to go in over the Bar for the night, as it was too rough to venture on to Bude, and a certain amount of fog added to the difficulty.

"At 8 o'clock I went below to rest for an hour, leaving the mate in charge. An hour later he came below to tell me there was water in the engine-room. I rushed to the engine-room and found the water being splashed about by the couplings of the engine. I was completely soaked, and as I entered the room I found the water almost up to my waist. I went on deck, and immediately manned the pumps until I was overtaken by exhaustion.

"Then the mate took over, while I went back to the engine-room, and found that the water, instead of decreasing, appeared to be higher than before We tried to get the ship in over the Bar, but the volume of water made her roll badly, and I gave orders for the ship's rowing boat to be launched.

33. Lead paragraphs, *Bideford Weekly Gazette*, 1st December 1936

KETCH'S 125 YEARS AT SEA

ESCAPES IN PEACE AND WAR

FROM OUR CORRESPONDENT

PLYMOUTH, Dec. 3

The foundering of the Bude ketch Ceres during fog in the Bristol Channel brought to an end the life of the oldest coasting vessel in service in the British Isles, and possibly in the world. The Ceres had traded around the coasts of England, Scotland, and Ireland for 125 years. Built at Salcombe in 1811, she was one of the heavily rigged fruit smacks which, fast for their size, plied between the West of England and Spain.

More than once she had narrow escapes from the attentions of French and American

The Ceres in Bude Harbour.

privateers. In the years 1813 and 1814 the British Government employed her to carry military stores to Wellington in the Peninsula. Her first visit to Bude was in 1826, when she arrived with a cargo of timber from Plymouth; but it was not until 1852 that she passed into the possession of Mr. Henry Petherick, of that port.

Having changed hands twice between 1811 and 1852, she was the property of the Petherick family for the remaining 84 years of her life. Mr. Henry Petherick's son, Mr. W. W. Petherick, became skipper in 1868. In December of that year, when she needed repair, he put the Ceres up on a slipway, cut her in half and lengthened her by 15ft., an operation which increased her carrying capacity from 52 to 85 tons.

"ALWAYS ALL THERE"

Her principal freights in those days were oats from Limerick to English Channel ports, but sometimes she traded to the Channel Islands and round to London and Ipswich, and at others to Liverpool and the West Coast. Mr. W. W. Petherick wrote of her 50 years ago: "We weathered out many storms in her, and she was always all there." He left the sea in 1884, and Mr. R. W. Petherick, his brother, became skipper. This member of the family spent 52 years in the Ceres, from the time he went to sea as a boy until 1928, when he retired. Mr. W. Stainton, who was in command from then until his death last July, had an association with the ketch, as boy, mate, and engineer, extending over 40 years. The last owner of the Ceres, Mr. A. Petherick, took her to sea on five occasions since last summer, although he was not on board on her last voyage.

Her closest call before the end came on November 7, 1900, when she was caught by a gale in Bude Bay, always a perilous lee-shore. That day a large Italian barque, the Concezione, which lay some distance to the windward of her, drifted on to the rocks about three miles below Bude, and became a total wreck. The Ceres, which had weathered many a blow in the bay, managed to make Padstow, but because of the force of the wind was unable to get right up harbour, and let both her anchors go. They dragged and she drifted

Continued in next column

on some rocks, where her crew jumped ashore. The ship's luck held even then. A tug not only took the crew off the rocks, but also towed the Ceres to safety.

GREAT STORM OF 1891

The old coaster rounded Land's End safely during the height of the great storm in March, 1891. Another vessel, running with her, was swept out into the Atlantic and could not make port for a week, and many big ships were cast ashore with grievous loss of life, while the Ceres struggled from Portmadoc to Plymouth with a cargo of slate.

During the War the Ceres, over 100 years old, ran the gauntlet of the German submarines which accounted for many coasting vessels, and traded regularly between Bude and the Bristol Channel ports. She seemed to have a charmed life. No harm ever came to her. For the hazards of Bude Bay, where hundreds of vessels have come to grief, she seemed to develop something like contempt. Although four or five years ago she had to heave-to for many hours off Trevose Head, she rode out the storm safely.

35. Front page of *The Toronto Evening Telegram*, 12th December 1936

Veteran of 125 Years at Sea
Ceres Lost on Active Service

From Our London Bureau,
By W. T. CRANFIELD,
Resident Staff Correspondent.

London. Dec. 12—Ceres, world's oldest ketch in active service, and oldest vessel registered at Lloyd's, has foundered in dense fog in Barnstable Bay.

In heavy weather, while bound from Swansea to Bude with a cargo of slag, she sprang a leak off dreaded Baggy Point, and so foundered as a good ship should, of her own infirmities, while pluckily going strong.

The skipper, Captain Oswald Jeffery, of Appledore, and the mate, Walter Ford, were saved by the Appledore lifeboat, after the two men had-worked the pumps until both were exhausted, and then lit flares as they entered the small boat of the sinking vessel.

Built at Salcombe, Devon, in 1811, the Ceres had been owned for the last 85 years by Petherick & Sons, of Bude.

Her career had elements of romance. During the Napoleonic wars she carried supplies, and had narrow escapes from French privateers. In the Great War she carried munitions. Once she was almost torpedoed.

Struggling to keep young, like all coquettish members of her sex, she had recently been fitted with a Diesel engine.

36. Copy of the original 1936 newspaper cutting

ii) Afterwards

Both Walter Ford, in his twenties, and Oswald Jeffery a few years older, were employed four months later, in the April of 1937, by the Pethericks, owners of the lost *Ceres*. Both seamen worked together once more, this time as mate and skipper of the *Traly*, the ketch purchased by the Pethericks to replace the *Ceres*. There was a great welcome for the *Traly* when she was brought into Bude that April.

37. Frank Clark, Walter Ford, Alfred Petherick,
Oswald Jeffery on the *Traly*, April 1937

Built in 1912, the *Traly,* previously a Braunton owned vessel and registered in Barnstaple, had been in the brick trade to Liverpool. The *Traly* was built of steel, had an 80hp engine, weighed 70 net registered tons and was able to carry 108 tons cargo, so she was somewhat larger than the *Ceres*, but still small enough to enter the harbour at Bude. Later on, probably in the early years of the Second World War, the *Traly* was sold to Norway and was in general trade in the Baltic under the name *Karma*. She subsequently reverted to her original name *Traly*, and as recently

8, 1937

New Motor Ketch For Bude

SHC
F
We

W

of union
Th
western
"Tw
to join
victimis
"H
the "hi
rapidly
organ

"D
will
of a
con
and
lep

for
bili-
ger
ngs
cil.
to
ffic

Visitors watching the berthing of Bude's new motor ketch Traly at the entrance to the canal. The Traly replaces the Ceres, which, when wrecked early this year, was the oldest vessel in Lloyd's Register

38. The welcome for the *Traly* on entering Bude in April 1937

as 1985 was known to still be working as a dredger out of Remmerstrand in Norway.

And Walter Ford and Oswald Jeffery? Well, both continued to follow the sea, a hard life but an interesting one, and both, as befitted old crewmen of the *Ceres,* died in bed on land. During the Second World War, Walter was given two shells and a small gun with which to defend the realm from the enemy off Appledore in his open, clinker built boat. This approach to repulsing an enemy at sea was just about as meaningless as that which was practised on board the *Ceres* one hundred and fifty years earlier. The brass casings from those two shells stood for many years one each side the kitchen range in the old family home at the top of One End Street, Appledore.

The *Ceres* meant a great deal to Walter Ford. It was the only vessel he ever talked to me about by name. Philip Ford of Appledore, (no relation), painted the *Ceres* entering Bude in the surf from Walter's framed photograph of her. That painting is reproduced on the cover of this book. He also painted, after Walter had died, a commemorative picture of the *Ceres* for Walter's widow, Beena. This tranquil painting has the *Ceres* heading out to sea from Appledore towards the Bar and into the sunset. Such gentle symbolism requires no explanation.

39. Commemorative watercolour of the *Ceres* leaving Appledore

Sources: articles, books, documents and unpublished work consulted

Articles:

1929: '*Ceres*. A wonderful record.' R. P. Hirst, in *Sea Breezes*, Vol XII, pps 206-207

1931: 'The Oldest Vessel Afloat' G. Mote, in *Ships and Ship's Models*, Vol 1, No.4 December

1934: Notes from the Editor's Chair, in *Sea Breezes*, Vol.XVIII, No.174

1937: 'The *Ceres*. Passing of Britain's Oldest Coasting Vessel,' J. G. Pierson, in *Sea Breezes*, Vol XXI, pps 294-295 Also see *Sea Breezes*, Vol XV, p245 (1947) and Vol XVI p303

Books:

1936: Third Edition: Capt. John E. Acland: *Budehaven*: Ferry Bolt Ltd, Bude

1966: Graham Farr: *Wreck and Rescue in the Bristol Channel*: D.Bradford Barton, Truro

1972: Helen Harris and Monica Ellis: *The Bude Canal*: David and Charles, Newton Abbot

1974: W. J. Slade and Basil Greenhill: *West Country Coasting Ketches*: Conway Maritime Press, Greenwich

1977: Rennie Bere: *The Story of Budehaven*: Bude-Stratton Town Council

1986: Gordon Mote: *The Westcountrymen*: Badger Books, Bideford, North Devon

2001: Bill Young and Bryan Dudley Stamp: *Bude's Maritime Heritage*: Bill Young, Bude

Documents:

1815-1816: Lloyd's Register, Guildhall Library, London
1817-1818: Lloyd's Register, Guildhall Library, London
1835: Lloyd's Register, National Maritime Museum, Greenwich
1927 to 1935: Cargo Book of the *Ceres*, Bude-Stratton Museum, Cornwall
1936: Mercantile Navy List, Guildhall Library, London

Unpublished:

Graham Farr: Card Index for *Ceres*, National Maritime Museum, Greenwich
Peter Walton: The Trade of the Port of Bude 1860-1927: Unpublished Thesis, Institute of Marine Studies, University of Plymouth
Bill Young: Notes for the *Ceres*
Michael Haydon: The Life of a Cornishman from Bude: Interview recorded by Phillipa Fitzpatrick, 18 January 1999
Ed Pethick: Interview conducted by John Bolitho and Phillipa Fitzpatrick, for the Bude, Stratton and District Old Cornwall Society, 23 November 2000
Oswald Jeffery: conversation about his father, Captain Oswald Jeffery, 2003
Nigel Astbury: conversation about jumboisation, 2004
Michael Pryce-Jones: conversation about asteroids, 2004
Barbara Allin, Jennifer Mills, Betty Wilson: conversation about slag, 2004

Acknowledgements:

Bude-Stratton Museum, Cornwall
Exeter City Library, Westcountry Studies Unit
National Maritime Museum, Greenwich
Guildhall Library, London
The Mitchell Library, Glasgow
Intellisearch, Toronto Reference Library, Canada
County Reference and Information Library, Truro, Cornwall
Cornish Studies Library, Redruth, Cornwall
Local Studies Unit, Barnstaple, North Devon
Northam Branch Library, North Devon
Mrs Phillipa Fitzpatrick, Museum Officer, Bude-Stratton Museum
Mrs George Wells, Walter Ford's daughter Ann
Julian Astbury, proof reader for final draft

Photographs, paintings and illustrations:

Watercolours used for front cover, and endpiece, courtesy of Mrs George Wells; also nos.1,2,4,5,13,14,30;
No 3, Graham Farr collection; No 6, Gordon Mote collection; Nos 7,8,10,11 Guildhall Library, London; No 12, National Maritime Museum, Greenwich;
Nos.16,37, records of the Bude, Stratton and District Old Cornwall Society. Nos.9,17,19,20,21,22,24,25,27,29 Bude-Stratton Museum;
No.15,23,28, the collections of Maurice Batley, John Pester, Mrs Lilian Herbert respectively;
Text illustrations, author.
News reports acknowledged in text.